THE PRACTICAL STRATEGIES SERIES
IN AUTISM EDUCATION

series editors
FRANCES A. KARNES & KRISTEN R. STEPHENS

Educational Strategies for Children With Autism Spectrum Disorders

Julie K. Ivey, Ph.D.

Routledge
Taylor & Francis Group

NEW YORK AND LONDON

First published 2009 by Prufrock Press Inc.

Published 2021 by Routledge
605 Third Avenue, New York, NY 10017
2 Park Square, Milton Park, Abingdon, Oxon OX14 4RN

Routledge is an imprint of the Taylor & Francis Group, an informa business

ISBN 13: 978-1-59363-371-4 (pbk)

Contents

Series Preface   1

Introduction   3

Strategies   5

General Techniques for Teachers   25

Conclusion   32

Resources   33

References   45

About the Author   48

The Practical Strategies Series in Autism offers teachers, counselors, administrators, parents, and other interested parties up-to-date information on a variety of issues pertaining to the characteristics, diagnosis, treatment, and education of students with autism spectrum disorders. Each guide addresses a focused topic and is written by an individual with authority on the issue. Several guides have been published. Among the titles are:

- *An Introduction to Children With Autism*
- *Diagnosis and Treatment of Children With Autism Spectrum Disorders*
- *Educational Strategies for Children With Autism Spectrum Disorders*

For a current listing of available guides within the series, please contact Prufrock Press at 800-998-2208 or visit http://www.prufrock.com.

The word autism is derived from the Greek word *autos* meaning *self*. Although cases of autism spectrum disorders (ASD) had been documented in the 18th century, Dr. Leo Kanner (1943) and Dr. Hans Asperger (1944/1991), independently of one another, were the first to systematically study the disorder in the 1940s. Today, autism and Asperger's syndrome have been combined with other disorders to fall under the continuum of autism spectrum disorders. This spectrum includes Autistic Disorder, Asperger's syndrome, Childhood Disintegrative Disorder, Rett's Disorder, and Pervasive Development Disorder-Not Otherwise Specified (PDD-NOS). Individuals with ASD exhibit a continuum of severity, ranging from mild to severe. In accordance with Drs. Kanner and Asperger, the current definition of an Autistic Disorder from the *Diagnostic and Statistical Manual for Mental Disorders: Fourth Edition* (*DSM-IV*; American Psychological Association, 1994) is (1) a qualitative impairment in social interaction; (2) a qualitative impairment in communication; and (3) restricted, repetitive, and stereotyped patterns of behavior, interests, and activities. These three impairments are often referred to as the triad or triangle of autistic disorders.

The impairment in social interactions can be seen by a lack of nonverbal behaviors such as eye contact, facial expressions, body postures, and typical social gestures. This impairment also is seen as an inability to form social relationships with peers and a seemingly lack of empathy. It is not that a child with autism does not care; it is that he or she has difficulty interpreting the perspectives of others. The impairment in communication skills can manifest itself from a total lack of verbal language to some simple word usage but with an inability to initiate or continue a conversation. A lack of imaginary or imitative play also is part of the communication impairment point of the autism triangle. Finally, the restricted, repetitive, and stereotyped behaviors appear as preoccupation of particular interests, inflexibility of transitioning to new activities or routines, and/or repetitive motor movements. Although not considered one of the points of the autism triangle, sensory or perceptual misrepresentations often accompany children with autism. This could include difficulties with certain sounds, tastes, touch, and the like.

According to the Centers for Disease Control and Prevention (CDC; 2008), in 2007 approximately 1 in 150 eight-year-old children had an ASD. It also is estimated that up to 560,000 children ages 0–21 currently have an ASD diagnosis with a male to female ratio of approximately 3:1. Children with autism almost always need special services in their school setting. It is projected that the United States serves more than 200,000 children classified with an ASD diagnosis in special education programs (CDC, 2008). Because autism spectrum disorders are on a continuum, educational placements can range from specialized autism classrooms to full-time inclusion in a general education classroom. It is important for teachers and staff to understand the various educational strategies that are available. It is the goal of this volume to provide interventions and strategies to help teachers and staff best serve students on the autism spectrum.

Applied Behavior Analysis

Applied Behavior Analysis (ABA) is the science of behavior. Catlett (2007) defined ABA as "the individualized systematic application of scientific principles of behavior to change specific, socially important behaviors within a format that includes continuous evaluation." Many people equate ABA with autism. Although ABA techniques and ideas are useful in working with children with autism, it is not solely used to treat autism. ABA techniques are used with every person, intentionally or not. In fact, ABA is not a methodology or a program; rather, it is a science involving the observation of behaviors and implementation of carefully designed strategies. When applying principles of ABA, the observer is charged with designing detailed, individualized treatment plans to affect a specific behavior. In addition, the observer is required to collect data for the purpose of designing a treatment plan and to follow the plan with continued data collection.

The practice of ABA involves several steps beginning with identification of the target behavior. After observing the child in several environments under varying conditions, a specific

Table 1
Antecedent/Consequence Function
of Behavior Data Collection Chart

Antecedent What happened just before?	Behavior What was the behavior?	Consequence What happened just after?

behavior is defined. Observers look for antecedents, or events occurring just prior to the specific behavior, and consequences, or events that take place just after the target behavior occurs. Antecedents and consequences are critical in determining the function of the behavior (see Table 1). The function of the behavior is what drives the child to act in a certain manner. By determining the function of a behavior, it is easier to answer questions like, "Why does he or she do that?" Functions of behavior include:
- escape/avoidance,
- attention,
- tangible/access, and
- sensory/internal.

Escape/Avoidance

Sometimes a student engages in a behavior with the intent to escape or avoid an undesirable demand. When confronted with a request that is unwanted, too difficult, or perceived to be too difficult, the child may behave in a way to get out of the situation. An example often seen in classrooms involves a teacher assigning students an activity to complete. If, for whatever reason, the student does not want to do the assignment, he may tantrum by yelling, falling to the floor, throwing things, or destroying property.

Table 2
Antecedent/Consequence Chart for
Escape/Avoidance Function of Behavior

Antecedent What happened just before?	Behavior What was the behavior?	Consequence What happened just after?
Teacher assigns activity	Student tears paper	Aide removes student

Often the child is removed from the classroom. In this instance, the adult teaches the child that throwing a tantrum is effective in getting out of the undesired demand. If the child is not successful in escaping the task completely, delaying the task is just as valuable. Arguing and negotiation often is a tactic useful in delaying a task. If the task is delayed long enough, it is possible that the teacher will give up, the bell will ring, or the teacher will change the assignment and make it easier. Ultimately the consequence is the same. Table 2 illustrates how an escape/avoidance function might be recorded on an antecedent/consequence chart.

Attention

Another function of behavior is attention. Social attention from an adult or peers is very rewarding to most children. Social attention can be in the form of laughter, affirmation, and reprimand. An example of attention-seeking behavior is the classic class clown. The class clown engages in silly behaviors to evoke a chuckle from classmates. Many times the teacher reprimands the student, further reinforcing the silly behavior. It is important to recognize that attention is valuable, whether it is positive in nature or not. Getting someone to attend to the student in any way is the goal. See Table 3 for an example of how an attention function of behavior is noted on antecedent/consequence chart.

Table 3
Antecedent/Consequence Chart for
Attention Function of Behavior

| Antecedent
What happened just
before? | Behavior
What was the
behavior? | Consequence
What happened just
after? |
|---|---|---|
| General classroom routines | Student makes armpit sounds | Peers laugh; teacher stops teaching to reprimand student |

Table 4
Antecedent/Consequence Chart for Tangible/Access
Function of Behavior

| Antecedent
What happened just
before? | Behavior
What was the
behavior? | Consequence
What happened just
after? |
|---|---|---|
| Child notices candy bar; parent says no | Child falls to the floor, kicks, and screams | Parent gives child candy bar |

Tangible/Access

A third function of behavior is to gain access to an activity or a tangible. The best example of this function can be seen in any grocery store checkout line. Imagine a mother checking out with her groceries. The child notices the vast array of candy and then hones in on a particular candy bar. The child sweetly asks the parent for the candy, to which the mother kindly replies, "No." The child falls to the floor, kicking and screaming. The mother, completely embarrassed, quickly gives the child the desired candy in an effort to stop the scene. What has the child learned?: Falling to the floor works well when attempting to gain a tangible. Table 4 details this form of function of behavior.

Table 5
Antecedent/Consequence Chart for Tangible/Access
Function of Behavior (School Example)

Antecedent What happened just before?	Behavior What was the behavior?	Consequence What happened just after?
Teacher calls for circle time	Student bangs instrument	Teacher sends student to computer

Perhaps a school example is appropriate. Imagine a child with a developmental disability in a self-contained classroom. The child really enjoys playing on the computer but the teacher insists that the student participate in a circle activity. The child refuses to participate and bangs an instrument on the floor. The teacher allows the student to play on the computer so the other students are not further disturbed (see Table 5 for sample documentation).

Sensory/Internal
The final function of behavior to be examined is for sensory purposes. People engage in behaviors stimulating a sensory response without awareness. Men who jingle the change in their pockets or women who tap their foot when their legs are crossed are engaging in self-stimulatory behaviors. See Table 6 for an example.

Each example in Tables 2–6 focuses on inappropriate behaviors; however, appropriate behaviors also can be used to achieve desired outcomes. Consider the child who raises her hand to gain the teacher's attention or one who asks for a break, explaining that the task is difficult. The purpose of determining the function of a particular behavior is to establish a treatment plan whereby the child can be taught appropriate replacement behaviors. By determining the function, the child can be taught how to obtain attention, escape a task, or gain access in a way that is socially

Table 6
Antecedent/Consequence Chart for Sensory/Internal
Function of Behavior (School Example)

Antecedent What happened just before?	Behavior What was the behavior?	Consequence What happened just after?
Student enters a noisy gym	Covers ears and moans in distress	Removal from gym to quiet environment

acceptable and functional. Without knowing the function, there is the danger of reinforcing an inappropriate behavior or not meeting the needs of students.

Applied behavior analysis is the attempt to determine why a behavior is occurring and to develop a socially appropriate plan to change the behavior. ABA is based on more than 30 years of research and relies on data collection to design, implement, and evaluate a treatment program.

The Developmental, Individual Difference, Relationship-Based (DIR®/Floortime™) Model

The Developmental, Individual Difference, Relationship-Based (DIR®/Floortime™) Model was created by child psychiatrist Dr. Stanley Greenspan. DIR® is a comprehensive approach that can include Floortime™, speech-language therapy, sensory integration therapy, a daily educational program, occupational therapy, peer-play opportunities, and biomedical treatments (Neisworth & Wolfe, 2005). This approach focuses on three areas:
- developmental—the six stages of child development,
- individual differences—processing of information in unique ways, and

- relationship-based—the learning that occurs within relationships (Greenspan & Wieder, 2006).

Floortime™, as one component of DIR®, is an intervention in which parents or therapists interact with children in a play setting for approximately 20–30 minutes per session. Floortime™ has two main goals: (1) to follow children's lead in order to understand and motivate them, and (2) to bring children into a shared world in order for them to be more empathetic, creative, logical, and reflective (Greenspan & Wieder, 2006). Once the child begins participating with the parent or therapist, he or she has an opportunity to work on relating, communicating, and thinking, while the parent or therapist is simultaneously encouraging maintaining of attention, relatedness, and two-way communication (Exkorn, 2005). For example, in their book *Engaging Autism: Using the Floortime Approach to Help Children Relate, Communicate, and Think*, Greenspan and Wieder provided a checklist for parents or therapists to use while facilitating floortime. Some of the points to consider are:
- Is the child engaging toys or me?
- Is the child reacting to or initiating conversations?
- Is the child labeling or creating new ideas?

Discrete Trial Training

Discrete Trial Training (DTT) is a teaching method that incorporates the practices of applied behavior analysis. DTT is more often associated with the treatment of children with autism spectrum disorders. Typically, DTT takes place in a one-on-one learning environment where the child and adult have limited distractions and the focus is on individualized, systematically planned objectives. The National Research Council (2001) suggested that children with autism require a sufficient amount of individual instruction to acquire objectives. The Council further suggested that discrete trial training, in combination with periods of structured teaching and incidental learning, could comprise an effective educational setting for children with autism.

DTT begins with a comprehensive assessment of the child's current level of functioning including academic, self-help, attentive, and behavior skills. After determining the current level of functioning, the instructor designs or follows a commercial curriculum designed to progress the student through a hierarchy of skills necessary for independence and growth. The skills include both academic and social skills and generally begin with attentive skills such as "look at me" and "hands down." The skills are divided into small discrete steps that build upon previous steps and are taught successively, ensuring mastery before progressing.

The process of discrete trial training involves three steps:

- cue,
- response, and
- consequence.

The completion of all three steps comprises a trial. First, the instructor places a demand on the student called a cue. The child responds either correctly or incorrectly. If the child responds correctly, the instructor immediately reinforces the behavior with a reward that has been determined to be reinforcing to the child. If the child answers incorrectly, the instructor repeats the cue and offers a prompt to ensure the child does not answer incorrectly again. Following the prompted answer, the child is not reinforced with a tangible, only a verbal praise. The instructor provides the same cue again and does not prompt. If, after the unprompted cue, the child answers correctly, the instructor then reinforces the correct behavior. This procedure is repeated multiple times until the child performs the task fluidly and without error. An example of this cue-response-consequence training is illustrated in Tables 7 and 8.

Discrete trial training is very effective in teaching new skills to students. It is important to remember that DTT is not intended to be used as an exclusive treatment for students with autism. Recent research has suggested children with autism must have opportunities to generalize skills, learned in one-on-one settings, to natural environments (Arick, Loos, Falco, & Krug, 2004). This con-

Table 7
Discrete Trial Training Chart: Example 1

Cue	Response	Consequence
"Do this" (teacher claps hands)	Student claps	Teacher gives student toy

Table 8
Discrete Trial Training Chart: Example 2

Cue	Response	Consequence
"Do this" (teacher claps hands)	Student jumps	Teacher does not respond
"Do this" (teacher claps hands)	Teacher assists student to clap hands	Teacher verbally praises
"Do this" (teacher claps hands)	Student claps hands	Teacher gives student toy

cept is made possible when teachers take advantage of incidental learning opportunities discovered throughout the routine of the daily structure. For example, children learning to identify colors in discrete trial training could generalize the skill by identifying colors during calendar time or recognizing their picture schedule of classroom activities by color coding the schedule. When used as part of a comprehensive program, discrete trial training is an effective and valuable teaching tool for students with autism.

Picture Exchange Communication System (PECS)

When entering school for the first time, many children with autism do not use speech to communicate (Bondy & Frost, 2002). The Picture Exchange Communication System (PECS) is not just about teaching a child to point at a picture. Often a child will point to a picture but be looking at something else, or have the ability to point to a picture but lack the initiation to approach the teacher. PECS is designed to teach functional communication with child initiation and no imitation.

The first step in PECS is to find out what is reinforcing to the child (e.g., toys, snacks). Once this is known, it can be used to teach the child to point to a picture of that item. This is done by using two people to work with the child. The first person sits in front of the child with the reinforcing item. As the child reaches for the item, the second person, sitting *behind* the child, guides the child's hand to pick up the picture of the item, reach toward the first person, and place the picture in his or her hand. The first person immediately gives the item to the child and says the object's name. It is important to note that there should be no speaking during this trial except for saying the object's name when given the picture. The first person should not ask things like, "What do you want?" and the second person should not say things like, "Let go of the picture." This first step may take awhile, but it is important for the child to learn it naturally with little assistance from the helpers.

The second step in PECS is to slowly increase the distance between the teacher with the reinforcement item and the child and the child and the pictures, and to increase the number of items a child can request. It is important to note here that if food was used as a reinforcer in the first step, a toy or some other item should be used in the second step. This is done to ensure that the child does not think that picture usage is only done at food or snack time. A communication binder, with Velcro on the inside to hold all of the pictures he or she may eventually be using, should be given to the child.

Once the child has learned how to effectively bring a picture to the teacher for a desired item, the third step is implemented to teach the child *which* picture to choose. This can be accomplished by introducing a new picture of a desired object, such as a cookie. When the child gives the teacher the desired picture, an actual cookie is given. The child will soon learn to differentiate between the two pictures and understand that randomly giving any picture will not result in a reward. To help speed up this process, feedback can be given. Although the teacher should not talk until he or she receives the picture, it is helpful to give positive or negative vocalizations (e.g., "uh-oh") as the child is reaching for either one of the pictures. Once two pictures can be discriminated, more pictures can be added, including similar items like sugar cookies and chocolate chip cookies. This can be demonstrated by giving the child a picture of each of the cookies. As the student hands the teacher one of the pictures, the teacher will then tell the child to go and get the cookie. If the correct cookie is chosen, the student is discriminating. If the wrong cookie is selected, the process can be repeated.

Although it is not within the scope of this section to continue any further with PECS, it can be expanded to teach picture sentence structure ("I want/yellow/crayons") and picture sentence answers ("Yellow/bear/gone"). It also can be continued to incorporate comments on how children feel and more.

Pivotal Response Treatments (PRT)

Pivotal Response Treatment (PRT) is used to work on three core areas of intervention: motivation to engage in social interactions and academics, the initiation of those interactions, and self-management (Koegel & Koegel, 2006). PRT is an intensive program that is used initially by the family (early intervention), but then by a combined effort of home and school. It is important for teachers to continue the PRT training that a child is receiving at home. Treatment must begin at an early age, be intensive (20–40 hours per week; National Research Council, 2001), and be delivered in natural environments (home and general education). The teacher's role is to work on communication skills and social interaction by focusing on motivation techniques in the curriculum. Motivating students to do their work requires both communication skills and social interaction.

It is important to note that a specialized curriculum is not being taught with this approach. Instead, the teacher will learn how to teach the general education curriculum to the child by focusing on motivation. The first step is to create a classroom environment with many choices of reinforcements and activities. This will ensure that students are reinforced for appropriate behavior and will allow them to choose desired activities. A few tips for teachers include using sound instructional techniques, having reinforcers entrenched everywhere throughout the day, preparing the child for changes in routine, watching for meltdown signs and knowing what to do when this happens, and creating a "safe place" for the child to go to if needed (Koegel & Koegel, 2006).

The next step is to modify the general education curriculum and motivate the student with ASD. A key point to remember is that a student does not have to do or learn the entire assignment in order to participate in it. It is important to focus on the parts of the assignment that you know the student can do and work from there. The following are guidelines, with examples, for modifying the curriculum (Koegel & Koegel, 2006).

1. *Identify which parts the student can do.* If a student can add two single digits together but cannot do three numbers, modify the assignment by providing the summation answer of two of the digits.

$$2 + 3 + 5 = ?$$

$$5$$

2. *Reinforce attempts.* Although students may not initially get the problem correct, reinforce their attempts and partially correct answers.

3. *Identify and limit the concepts to learn.* If the class assignment is to match a group of words to their common classification group and a student with ASD has trouble reading, make his or her goal for the assignment be to correctly read each of the words instead of classifying them.

4. *Provide orientation clues.* If the assignment is to do a word search in a grid-box of letters, and the student is lost in the maze of letters, modify the word box so that all of the words read

left to right and write out the word he or she is to find in the same row outside the box that contains the word.

5. *Make the task more concrete.* If the class is learning fractions and looking at pie charts that are variously shaded, you can make this more concrete for a student with ASD. This can be done by writing next to the pie chart "shaded parts _____" and directly under that write "total parts _____". The student then fills out the blanks and then can visually see the fraction he or she made.

6. *Make the activity more relevant to your student's interests and experiences.* This is important for all students too. Using examples (e.g., computers, airplanes, or nature) that students have experienced or like enhances the learning experience.

7. *Provide peer interaction within the activities.* Allow other children to work together with the student with ASD to show him or her how to do things. Reward all children appropriately.

Remember, the goal of modifying the curriculum is to help students with ASD achieve and learn new concepts without overwhelming them. It is not to be modified so much that the students are not motivated to learn anything new.

Finally, self-management can be taught to students to increase their motivation for socially appropriate behaviors and communication. First, children with ASD need to be taught what is appropriate and what is not. It is necessary to start only with one negative behavior to work on so as not to overwhelm students. Using reinforcers can help accomplish this goal. When the students are doing the appropriate response, reward them; when they are not, take away the reward. Next, they may begin to learn to tally intervals of appropriate behavior. For a child who is yelling out every 30 seconds, the interval for rewarding behavior should start at 10 seconds. This will establish a positive support of appropriate behavior. The interval time can then be expanded to minutes, hours, days, and so forth. Although the teacher should occasionally monitor the children's self-management, it is important to allow students to become autonomous. If you are concerned about students falsely filling out their self-management tallies, you can fill out the same form and reward them for completing it accurately.

Sensory Integration Therapy

The key concept to understand in sensory integration therapy is that normally developing children have a balance within and between their senses. That is, a child's sense of touch, taste, sight, hearing, and body position are all within normal limits. A hot stove feels hot, but a warm stove just feels warm. However, children who have a developmental disorder such as autism can have serious sensory issues. The brains of children with autism can misinterpret the sensory signals they are receiving from their environment (Arnwine, 2007). In comparison to the previous example, a warm stove might actually feel like a hot stove to a child with autism.

There are three ways a child can have sensory issues. The first is a hyperreactive response. Children with autism who are hyperreactive may interpret basic safe environmental stimuli as being incredibly painful or harmful. They may cover their ears or scream when they hear small noises or keep away from people for fear of being touched. The second way children may have sensory problems is a hyporeactive or underreactive response. In this situation, children need more stimulation from the environment because they are not getting enough. They may seem unaware of cuts or bruises, or continually chew on inedible objects they find around. The final way children can have a sensory issue is a combination of hyper- and hyporeactive responses. They may be hyperreactive to some stimuli and hyporeactive to other stimuli. It is important to be aware of and understand which sensory issues a child exhibits.

A sensory diet (Arnwine, 2007) is like any other diet that a body needs. Children who are hyporeactive to touch and need to constantly smear paint on the wall do not simply need to be told to stop, but instead should be given alternative and appropriate touch sensations to feed their sensory needs. Alternatively, children who are hyperreactive to touch may shy away from people and avoid everything. However, such children still need some sensory input in their daily diet, and it is important not to "starve" them by just leaving them alone. Instead, they should be given some pleasing sensory experiences.

The following activities can be used for children with sensory needs. The child's occupational therapist (OT) should be consulted before applying any of these activities to help tailor them to specifically fit the child's needs (Arnwine, 2007).

Hyporeactive Activities
Touch:
- Children who are not getting enough touch stimulation and like to paint may use the paint on inappropriate places. A substitute for paint can be unscented shaving cream that has food coloring in it. They can rub and paint with it and clean-up is easy. In addition, the shaving cream acts as a cleanser itself, and can help clean up other stains.
- Children who enjoy touching and squeezing objects and may become distracted by that need can be given small balloons that are filled with sand, salt, rice, and/or flour (squishies) to hold and squeeze during lesson times. Some children may prefer to use the shaving cream paint and splatter paint with the squishy.

Visual:
- Children who require large amounts of visual stimuli can be quickly distracted by all of the things in a classroom. If children are allowed a few minutes to receive that visual stimuli (when appropriate), they may be calmed.
- Allow children to use color overlays for written assignments. The use of posters in the classrooms can assist with visual attention.

- Allow children to play with a light toy during specific times, or poke a number of holes in a cereal box and put a flashlight in the box. The "stars" will come out.

Auditory:
- Children who desire noise to feed their stimulation needs may resort to banging on classroom objects. Playing soothing music during the day will meet their auditory needs and can help the teacher relax.
- You may want to set up a pot and pan drum set in another room. Allow them to bang away for a few minutes before returning to class.

Hyperreactive Activities
Touch:
- Children who don't like to be touched still need touch stimulation to continue their development. Start slow; use a cotton ball to touch them on their hands, arms, and face. Once they are comfortable with that, touching can involve harder objects and eventually they should be able to shake hands.

Visual:
- Children who are sensitive to the light can be incredibly uncomfortable in the classroom. Dim the lights or let them wear lightly tinted sunglasses inside and darker tinted glasses outside at recess.

Auditory:
- Sensitivity to sounds can be difficult for some children due to the random noises in the classroom and the occasional fire drill. Play soothing music during the day but start at a very quiet volume. Gradually turn up the volume a little bit each day or every week until it reaches a comfortable level.

- A great strategy to use that allows children to make noise is object hiding. During a break, have a child hide an object in the room. The child is to clap or bang louder and louder as the teacher gets closer to the object and softer as the teacher gets further from the object.

These strategies are only a few of the myriad of ideas for these senses and the others, including smell and gross and fine motor sensory perception that can be found in books such as Arnwine's (2007) *Starting Sensory Integration Therapy*.

Social Stories™

Carol Gray created Social Stories™ as a way for children with autism spectrum disorders to learn social skills (Exkorn, 2005). Social Stories™ are short stories written by a parent, teacher, or therapist that address a specific skill, situation, or behavior. The story gives information about an event, such as *where, when, who* will be involved, and *why,* as a means of preparing the student for the situation (Neisworth & Wolfe, 2005). The story also gives important cues about desired behavior or reactions. The stories are written for a specific situation and are customized to the needs of the child.

The Social Stories™ concept can be used in a classroom to teach a variety of subjects, including conversation skills (e.g., initiating and maintaining conversation), proper classroom behavior (e.g., standing in line or raising hands), and social skills (e.g., when to say please and thank you and how to share; Luiselli, Russo, Christian & Wilczynski, 2008). The stories are simple, do not include many sentences, typically have simple drawings, and target one skill. Teachers can create Social Stories™ relatively quickly and then reuse them to reinforce desired behavior or skills.

TEACCH

Treatment and Education of Autistic and related Communication-handicapped Children (TEACCH) was created by Dr. Eric Schopler during the 1960s. Schopler refuted the current opinion of the causes of autism and developed a "culture of autism," which became a foundation model for understanding the condition. The culture of autism refers to the differences between individuals with and without autism and recognizes them as differences rather than disabilities. Specifically, people with autism think and learn differently and have differences in neurobehavioral patterns. TEACCH recognizes that children with ASD think differently in that they focus on details; are distractible; and have difficulty with abstract concepts, integration of ideas, and organization. Differences in learning are evident as children with autism generally are visual learners and easily become prompt dependent. Additionally, children with autism have strong impulses and experience excessive levels of anxiety. Finally, autism tends to create differences in sensory and perceptual processing. It is through recognition and acknowledgement of these differences that developers created the process of structured teaching.

Mesibov, Shea, and Schopler (2006) wrote *The TEACCH Approach to Autism Spectrum Disorders* in which the TEACCH model is described from its inception to current-day practice. The mission of TEACCH is to create a learning environment whereby the visual strengths of students with autism are acknowledged and used in such a way as to make the child successful in school. Structured teaching involves many steps on a pyramid model. The base of the pyramid begins by infusing physical structure into a learner's environment. Either through the use of natural components of the classroom (e.g., bookshelves or cabinets) or by using constructed barriers, the classroom is arranged to provide structure for the student. Specific learning areas in the room are delineated from others and defined in their purpose. Second, students are taught to use schedules in an effort to reduce anxiety by informing the student of events to come.

Third, the student's work is organized in a system that allows the child to know exactly what is expected during the activity. Fourth, students are taught routines that are learned naturally by typically developing children but must be taught specifically to children with ASD. Finally, work tasks are organized for children in such a way as to answer four critical questions:

- What work must I do?
- How much work must I complete?
- How do I know when I am finished?
- What do I do next?

Tasks that answer these four questions are structured in such a way that children with autism can successfully complete work assignments.

TEACCH prefers to address behavior using an iceberg model. The tip of the iceberg is all that is visible to the eye. However, it is known that there is much that exists below the surface. TEACCH proposes one should look beyond the tip of the iceberg represented by the abhorrent behavior displayed by the child and determine what below the surface is causing the inappropriate behavior. TEACCH posits that it is the characteristics of autism below the surface that cause the behaviors and one must address interventions concerning these autism characteristics in order to effect change. Interventions usually include structuring the environment, lessening anxiety by using a visual schedule, and increasing language by using TEACCH methodologies.

TEACCH recognizes the importance of communication and makes it a pivotal piece of teaching and learning in the model. Teachers are trained to individualize instruction beginning with a communication assessment. Teachers use the principles of scaffolding in which knowledge the student already possesses becomes the foundation for teaching new, unfamiliar language. For nonverbal children, the TEACCH model uses line drawings, pictures, and written words to provide opportunities for communication. Additionally, conversational skills, topic selection, turn-taking and staying on topic are addressed with children who have verbal communication skills.

Social skills are an integral part of the TEACCH model as most children with ASD behave very differently than children without autism. Training is based upon a social skills assessment and addresses differences in skills such as proximity, sharing, initiation, turn-taking, rule following, and interfering behaviors. As often as possible, the interest of the student is taken into consideration when developing a plan to teach social skills. Training takes place either in highly structured group settings or individually. Many times, typical peers are included in the training process and serve as excellent role models for students with ASD.

Auditory Integration Therapy

Auditory Integration Therapy (AIT) was developed by Dr. Guy Berard, an ear, nose, and throat specialist, in order to rehabilitate hearing loss (Exkorn, 2005). AIT has since been used with children who have ASD as a type of auditory training with the intent of improving listening skills, language competency, and overall auditory processing (Exkorn, 2005; Neisworth & Wolfe, 2005). The therapy begins with a hearing exam that examines the frequencies to which the child is hypersensitive. Then during two, half-hour sessions per day for 10 days, the child listens to music for which the identified frequencies are either filtered out or altered in order to strengthen the middle ear (Neisworth & Wolfe, 2005). Proponents claim that this method reduces hypersensitivity to sounds and prevents sensory overload (Exkorn, 2005; Neisworth & Wolfe, 2005). A decrease in impulsivity also has been reported by parents as a result of AIT, although further research is recommended in this area (Exkorn, 2005).

Interactive Metronome Therapy

An individual's ability to feel and produce a beat, called his or her mental interval timekeeping or simply "timing," has been shown to relate to performances in music, sports, speech-communication, and mathematics and reading achievement (Kuhlman & Schweinhart, 1999; Taub, McGrew, & Keith, 2007). Metronomes, invented in 1696 by Etienne Loulie, have made it possible for individuals to estimate their accuracy in keeping time with music and movement (Shaffer et al., 2001). Another type of metronome, The Interactive Metronome, was invented in 1992 and is a product of Synaptec, LLC, of Grand Rapids, MI (Shaffer et al., 2001). This is a PC-based metronome that uses technology to more precisely measure an individual's timing (Kuhlman & Schweinhart, 1999; Shaffer et al., 2001). Through the use of motion-sensing triggers placed either on the hand or foot, participants work through a series of exercises, such as patting their knee with their hands, toe-tapping, or walking in place as the computer records the accuracy of how the participant keeps in time during the tasks (Kuhlman & Schweinhart, 1999; Shaffer et al., 2001). The system is interactive in that participants are able to immediately make changes in their rhythm or timing according to the feedback from the program. The program typically consists of 15 one-hour sessions, held over the course of a few weeks (Shaffer et al., 2001).

One objective of Interactive Metronome Therapy is to "help participants improve their ability to selectively attend, without interruption by internal thoughts or external distractions, for extended periods of time" (Shaffer et al., 2001, p. 158). The therapy also has been positively correlated with gains in broad reading, reading fluency, attention, motor control, language processing, and academic performance (Kuhlman & Schweinhart, 1999; Shaffer et al., 2001; Taub et al., 2007).

Modeling

Imitation, which is a result of modeling, is a very important skill that children use to learn about their environment. Children with ASD often have severe deficits in imitating others and this can be cause for concern as they cannot learn by watching others. Therefore, it is important to help train a child with ASD to imitate. One strategy to use is modeling lessons or activities by their peers. When teaching students to imitate, make sure it is something they enjoy doing and reward them for correctly imitating (e.g., if they like to draw, have them imitate drawing particular objects). Once the student has begun to learn how to imitate, he or she can be modeled and taught more complex behaviors such as appropriate social interactions. It is at this point that video modeling has great benefits. First, the student with autism can watch a video about correct social interactions, and then he or she can watch it again, seeing it exactly the same way it happened the first time. This exact repetition will enhance the student's learning. Also, the student with autism can be video-taped using appropriate behaviors and then shown the video to demonstrate another perspective. There are many DVDs currently available (see Resources section in this volume) that have modeling activities that include everything from saying hello and raising your hand, to developing social skills and friendships.

Music Therapy

Music therapy is an approach that uses music to accomplish nonmusical goals. It is based on studies that have shown children with ASD "respond more frequently, more appropriately and with more pleasure to music than to any other auditory stimulus" (Coleman, 2005, p. 191). The therapy begins with a board-certified music therapist (MT-BC) assessing a child, either by test items or observation; creating goals and objectives specific to the child; and then planning a means with which to measure the therapy's effectiveness (King, 2004). Music therapists also can collaborate with parents, teachers, therapists, or other professionals as part of a team approach (Coleman, 2005).

Music therapy can provide a stimulating environment that promotes physical, cognitive, communication, social, or emotional development (Neisworth & Wolfe, 2005). For example, participants have the opportunity to practice motor skills, taking turns, and sharing while using instruments (Coleman, 2005). The environment also encourages communication through practice of singing or listening skills. In addition, the therapy can focus more on academic skills, such as learning or practicing the multiplication table in a musical format.

Peer Mentoring

Peer mentoring is an excellent way to help teach a student with ASD. Not only is it beneficial to the mentee, but it also teaches valuable skills to the mentor. The first step in creating a mentorship for a student is to pick a mentor who can and will get along with the student with ASD. Next, ask the possible mentor if he or she would like to participate. This mentorship must be voluntary, as forcing a child to mentor would not be beneficial. Once you have a student on board it is important to explain to him or her why it is important to be a mentor. Explain to the mentor that the child with ASD needs help with learning. This can be difficult and, depending on the student's age, a detailed explanation may not be needed. Finally, introduce the mentor to the student and have the mentor explain to the student that he or she is there to help the student. There are then three simple steps to the actual mentoring process: (1) demonstration, (2) corrective feedback, and (3) descriptive praise. The following is an example of a mentorship session.

> Carl: Hi Lenny, I am going to help you learn how to shake hands today. Is that OK?

> Lenny: Yes.

Carl: (Demonstration) First, you put your hand out like this, then when the other person puts his hand out, you put them together like this, then you gently squeeze. Pretty cool, huh? Now you try it.

(Lenny tries to initiate it, but incorrectly.)

Carl: (Corrective feedback) Oh, that was close but make sure you put your hand out farther. Let's try it again.

(Lenny correctly initiates and concludes a handshake.)

Carl: (Descriptive praise) That was perfect! I really liked how gently you squeezed my hand and that you didn't hang on for too long.

It is important that the descriptive praise be descriptive. Don't just have them say, "good job, that's right" but have them specifically point out details about what was right. Although this is a simplistic example it should give you a general idea of the three steps.

Visual Cues

Teachers of students with autism can develop a checklist or chart for students to follow. This will allow students to complete classroom tasks (e.g., classroom activities, responsibilities/duties, assignments). Students can chart their own record of on-task behavior and tasks that are completed. Students with ASD often can benefit from holding an object to help them stay focused while performing a task. The teacher and student can agree on the sensory object beforehand. One should maintain visibility with the student, as the teacher and student should be able to see each other. It is important to make eye contact possible at all times. Books can be utilized to teach visual attention. Allowing the student to choose a book of interest and having the student identify times when the character is using appropriate visual attention can be beneficial. Developing contracts with students written within their ability level and focusing on one behavior at a time can be helpful, specifically when they emphasize what behavior is expected (e.g., concentrating on a task) and what reinforcement will be made available when the terms of the contract have been met. In addition, allowing the student to underline or highlight important information he or she reads (e.g., directions, reading assignments) will help to facilitate concentration.

Teachers should keep in mind that students with ASD can feel overstimulated with visual distractions. For example, students may need to have the amount of information on a page reduced (e.g., less print to read, fewer problems, isolated information that is presented to the student). Make certain that only those materials necessary for performing the task are on the student's desk (e.g., pencil, textbook, paper). Additional materials such as a library book or scissors may distract the student. Teachers also can help reduce visual distractions by moving the student away from doors, windows, and busy hallways. In addition, carrels or dividers can be used to reduce visual stimuli. Students can wear UV protecting glasses if they feel that the light is too bright inside and outside. Finally, discuss with students their feelings and perceptions when they become overwhelmed. Teach them that individuals perceive things differently. Educate students on all strategies and tools available across environments and settings to decrease sensitivity.

Play

Because students with ASD often have difficulty with social skills, prefer to play alone, and have difficulty making friends, teachers and staff may need to provide interventions in this domain. Teachers can explicitly teach age-appropriate leisure skills (e.g., sports skills, board games, rules of ball games). These skills do not always come naturally. Students with ASD can practice social skills and develop regular conversations to use at different times (e.g., "Hi, My name is ___. Would you like to play?") Developing, with the student, a list of high-interest, leisure activities that require various amounts of time to perform and involve other kids (e.g., game of checkers, Boy/Girl Scouts, dance class) could be beneficial. In addition, providing organized activities on the playground, such as four square, tetherball, jump rope, and softball, can be helpful. Teachers can implement a weekly social skill lesson into the classroom curriculum. This will encourage friendships and also help students practice social skills (e.g., shaking hands, using manners, maintaining eye contact). Teachers can reward students for participation in group situations and even provide frequent opportunities to meet new people, such as allowing students to run errands with a peer to facilitate interaction or assigning one or two peers to work together on a long-term project. One also can model appropriate ways to respond to interactions with other students and teachers. Keep in mind that "pushing" the student too hard when encouraging interaction may cause the student to become frightened or withdrawn. Offering opportunities for positive reinforcement from socializing rather than to "demand" a display of social skills is a far better approach.

Conclusion

Many children are increasingly being diagnosed with ASD. With this increase there are additional concerns regarding quality of education and the influence of teachers on these students. Teacher expectations affect many aspects of the academic life of children with autism spectrum disorders. Their expectations determine the amount and quality of effort exerted toward the students' needs. According to Ivey (2007), teachers are positive about their students' success in the classroom. That optimistic outlook, along with the focused strategies and beneficial information in this book, will go a long way toward ensuring success in the classroom as well as confidence in children with autism spectrum disorders.

Books/Workshop

Albert, P. A., & Troutman, A. C. (2006). *Applied behavior analysis for teachers* (7th ed.). Upper Saddle River, NJ: Prentice Hall. This book is used as a textbook in many college education courses. It is very useful in describing the principles of applied behavior analysis as applicable to teachers. The text is easy to read and full of valuable tools for collecting and analyzing data and implementing strategies.

Arick, J. R., Loos, L., Falco, R., & Krug, D. A. (2004). *The STAR Program: Strategies for teaching based on autism research.* Austin, TX: Pro-Ed.
The STAR Program is an invaluable curriculum for teachers of students with low to moderate autism spectrum disorders. The curriculum includes assessments, instructions, lessons, and manipulatives necessary to teach students expressive and receptive language, functional routines, and play and social skills, as well as academic skills. The program is based in sound research and implements strategies of applied behavior analysis.

Arnwine, B. (2007). *Starting sensory integration therapy.* Arlington, TX: Future Horizons.
This book is a very practical and useful guide to developing sensory activities for your child. Multiple ideas for all five senses plus fine and gross motor activities are explored.

Berard, G. (2000). *Hearing equals behavior.* Chicago: Keats.
A clear and simple book on the theory that even minute distortions in hearing can affect how one acts. Berard discusses the scientific function of hearing and the treatment that can help children with learning disabilities, dyslexia, and autism.

Bondy, A., & Frost, L. (2002). *A picture's worth: PECS and other visual communication strategies in autism.* Bethesda, MD: Woodbine House.
PECS is an excellent guide for developing a communication system using pictures. Step-by-step instructions are given to develop this skill.

Catlett, S. M. (2007, August). *De-mystifying applied behavior analysis (ABA).* Workshop conducted for Belton ISD, Belton, TX.
Susan Catlett provides extensive research-based professional development. Information from her workshop educates the attendee about fundamentals of applied behavior analysis. Catlett serves primarily the Houston area; however, she reaches audiences across the state of Texas and nationally. She can be reached through Autism Consultation and Education, Inc.; 5426 Windham Springs Court; Houston, TX 77041; Phone: (713) 686-8713.

Coleman, M. (2005). *The neurology of autism.* New York: Oxford University Press.
This book focuses on the neurological signs and symptoms of autism and provides current medical, educational, and alternative therapies available. Topics include epilepsy, cranial circumference, changes in muscle tone, and mutism found in children with autism.

Exkorn, K. S. (2005). *The autism sourcebook: Everything you need to know about diagnosis, treatment, coping and healing.* New York: Collins.

This book helps to explain and guide parents through the diagnosis, treatment, coping, and healing stages. Topics include understanding and accessing treatment options, coping with marital or family stress, and understanding your child's behaviors. The book also contains a list of Internet resources, a glossary of common terms, and information about international organizations for autism.

Gray, C. (2000). *The new social stories book: Illustrated edition.* Arlington, TX: Future Horizons.

This illustrated book has multiple social stories to help children with autism learn new skills. Topics range from how to give a hug, to how to deal with nightmares, and much more. Each story is accompanied with suggestions on how parents and teachers can modify the story to best fit their child's needs.

Greenspan, S. I., & Wieder, S. (2006). *Engaging autism: Using the floortime approach to help children relate, communicate, and think.* Cambridge, MA: De Capo Press.

This book explains the Developmental, Individual-Difference, Relationship-Based (DIR®/Floortime™) Model, including how families can use this model to promote relating, communicating, and thinking with their children. An explanation and application of the Floortime™ technique also is included as well as a section on overcoming difficult symptoms such as self-stimulation and toilet training.

King, B. (2004). *Music therapy: Another path to learning and communication for children on the autism spectrum.* Arlington, TX: Future Horizons.

This resource book explains the theory of music therapy as well as the qualifications of a music therapist, the therapeutic characteristics of music, and how to achieve nonmusical goals through this therapy. The book has many examples of songs or activities that are used in music therapy.

Koegel, R. L., & Koegel, L. K. (2006). *Pivotal response treatments for autism*. Baltimore: Brookes.
This book is an extensive resource for pivotal response treatments. It includes strategies and theories for parents, teachers, and others to promote this intensive program. Reinforcement, curriculum modification, and self-management are only some of the areas explored.

Lord, C., & McGee, J. P. (Eds.). (2001). *Educating children with autism*. Washington, DC: National Academy Press.
This book was written to provide a compilation of "scientific evidence concerning the effects and features of educational interventions for young children with autism" (p. 2). After extensive research and data collection, effective educational interventions regarding every aspect of a child's life was integrated into a single publication.

Luiselli, J. K., Russo, D. C., Christian, W. P., & Wilczynski, S. M. (2008). *Effective practices for children with autism: Educational and behavioral support interventions that work*. New York: Oxford University Press.
This resource book has in-depth information about various educational and behavioral interventions. Included interventions are ABA, developmental play, naturalistic teaching, antecedent intervention, and many others. Topics such as staff training, family support, and effective educational programs also are included.

Mesibov, G. B., Shea, V., & Schopler, E. (2006). *The TEACCH approach to autism spectrum disorders*. New York: Springer Science+Business Media, LLC.
This book is a step-by-step explanation of the fundamental beliefs of the TEACCH model. The TEACCH model is explained in detail from its inception to its current use in classrooms.

Neisworth, J. T., & Wolfe, P. S. (2005). *The autism encyclopedia.* Baltimore: Brookes.

This reference guide is a compilation of more than 500 terminologies related to autism. It also includes a section on screening and assessment tools and curricula as well as a section on various government agencies and advocacy organizations.

Web Sites

Auditory Integration Training
http://www.aitresources.com
This is the Web site of Michael and Marcy McCarthy, practitioners of Auditory Integration Training (AIT). It provides a history of AIT and information regarding AIT candidacy, outcomes, and tests.

Auditory Integration Training
http://www.aitresources.com
Auditory Integration Training is considered an alternative, nonpharmaceutical, noninvasive intervention designed to alleviate hearing discomfort or hypersensitivity. It has been known to accelerate progress with allied therapies such as speech, occupational therapy, movement, and other developmental therapies. DAN (Defeat Autism Now) doctors advise parents to consider AIT as one of the first interventions to alleviate symptoms of autism, reduce painful hearing (hyperacusis), and improve receptive language.

Autism Research Institute
http://www.autism.com
The Autism Research Institute conducts research and disseminates research-based information on methods of diagnosing and treating autism.

Autism Collaboration

http://www.autism.org

This Web site is a collaborative of autism advocacy organizations focused on initiating parent-driven research initiatives.

The National Autistic Society

http://www.autism.org.uk

This is a leading organization in the United Kingdom dedicated to supporting individuals with autism and their families.

Healing Thresholds

http://autism.healingthresholds.com

This is a Web site that connects parents with autism therapy information.

AutismLink

http://www.autismlink.com

This site provides a link to individual states' autism resources. There is also a chat room, provider database, and a mentor program. A great site designed to help you find resources in your area.

Autism Research Network

http://www.autismresearchnetwork.org/AN

This Web site provides information on the two, NIH-supported research networks that focus on understanding and treating autism.

Autism Society of America

http://www.autism-society.org

This Web site is a member-based organization that allows for involvement on many different levels. A great place to start learning about autism, including diagnosis and treatment.

Autism Speaks

http://www.autismspeaks.org

Autism Speaks aims to bring the autism community together as one strong voice to urge the government and private sector to listen to its concerns and take action to address this urgent global health crisis. The site is dedicated to funding global biomedical research into the causes, prevention, treatments, and cure for autism.

AutismSpot
http://www.autismspot.com
This site provides a free and unbiased resource for the autism community. It captures best practices, therapies, various education opportunities, resources, tools, and home program ideas from around the world and presents them in a video format that is current, relevant, and easily accessible.

Cambridge Center for Behavioral Studies
http://www.behavior.org/autism
At this Web site you will find information about the causes of autism and the Applied Behavior Analysis (ABA) treatment approach.

Centers for Disease Control and Prevention—Autism Information Center
http://www.cdc.gov/ncbddd/autism
This is the Centers for Disease Control and Prevention's information Web site on autism. It includes information on vaccines, diagnosis, treatment, and current statistics on autism.

Autism Research Institute
http://www.defeatautismnow.com
This organization offers conferences that provide the latest information for parents and professionals on the causes and treatment of autism.

DisabilityInfo.gov
http://www.disabilityinfo.gov
This is an online resource that provides access to information regarding disability programs, services, laws, and benefits to individuals with disabilities and their families.

First Signs

http://www.firstsigns.org

This is a nonprofit organization dedicated to raising awareness of the early warning signs of autism.

The Interdisciplinary Council on Developmental and Learning Disorders (ICDL)

http://www.icdl.com

The organization integrates knowledge from different disciplines to help improve our understanding of autism. An abundance of information regarding the DIR®/Floortime™ Model is available at this Web site.

Pyramid Educational Consultants

http://www.pecs.com

Home of the Picture Exchange Communication System (PECS), this consulting firm offers a wide array of products and services for parents and educators.

Polyxo.com

http://www.polyxo.com

This site offers a wealth of information related to instructional techniques appropriate for children with autism.

Tammy Glaser

http://home.earthlink.net/~tammyglaser798/authome.html

A personal Web site that reveals the world of an inspirational family that has overcome many obstacles.

TEACCH Autism Program

http://www.teacch.com

A service, training, and resource program whose mission is to help individuals with autism lead meaningful, independent lives.

The Gray Center
http://www.thegraycenter.org
Directed by Carol Gray, the creator of Social Stories™, this organization works to improve social understanding by helping individuals with autism communicate more successfully.

Wrightslaw
http://www.wrightslaw.com
This Web site is a comprehensive source of information regarding special education law and advocacy for individuals with disabilities.

DVDs

Autism Research Centre (Firm), & Harcup, C. (Executive
    Producer). (2006). *The transporters* [DVD]. Cambridge,
    England: Changing Media Development.
Developed with the Autism Research Centre at Cambridge
University, this DVD uses animated vehicles with real human
faces to help children transfer learning to real life.

Brandissimo. (2005). *Spectrum connections. Vol. 1, Connecting emo-
    tions* [DVD]. Encino, CA: Author.
This DVD features original songs and activities that help children
identify and coordinate basic emotions and physical activities.
The DVD includes added features and information for parents.

Brandissimo. (2005). *Spectrum connections: Vol. 2, Connecting body
    movement* [DVD]. Encino, CA: Author.
Spectrum Connections is all about connections, connecting children
with autism to their own thoughts, words, and actions, as well as
connecting children with autism with their parents. The DVD
features original songs and activities targeted to help children
identify and model a variety of physical gestures and concepts.

Educational Products for Infancy. (2003). *Bee smart baby: Action
    words, volume 2* [DVD]. Crystal Beach, FL: Baby Bumblebee.
This DVD will help a child learn specific action words to use
in everyday situations. With every word clearly illustrated, this
DVD will provide hours of entertainment and education.

Model Me Kids. (2005). *I can do it! For children with autism, Asperger
    syndrome, PDD-NOS, nonverbal learning disorders, social anxiety,
    learning disabilities and delays* [DVD]. Rockville, MD: Author.
Models appropriate behavior in stressful situations, including
waiting, transitions, birthday parties, handling criticism, and
more.

Model Me Kids. (2005). *Time for a playdate: For children with autism, Asperger syndrome, PDD-NOS, nonverbal learning disorders, social anxiety, learning disabilities and delays* [DVD]. Rockville, MD: Author.

This DVD includes topics such as greeting a friend, losing, answering, playing a friend's way, making eye contact, cleaning up, saying goodbye, and more.

Model Me Kids. (2005). *Time for school: For children with autism, Asperger syndrome, PDD-NOS, nonverbal learning disorders, social anxiety, learning disabilities and delays* [DVD]. Rockville, MD: Author.

This DVD includes topics such as listening to the teacher, sharing, sitting quietly, taking turns, showing interest in others, playing on the playground, and more.

Model Me Kids. (2007). *Model me conversation cues: For children with autism, Asperger syndrome, PDD-NOS, nonverbal learning disorders, social anxiety, learning disabilities and delays* [DVD]. Rockville, MD: Author.

Models nonverbal cues, how and when to start a conversation, how to maintain conversation, turn-taking in conversation, and more.

Model Me Kids. (2007). *Model me friendship: For children with autism, Asperger syndrome, PDD-NOS, nonverbal learning disorders, social anxiety, learning disabilities and delays* [DVD]. Rockville, MD: Author.

Models social skills involved in initiating and maintaining a friendship including: compromise, invite, handling rejection, team sports, empathy, and more.

Model Me Kids. (2008). *Model me tips & tricks: For children with autism, Asperger syndrome, PDD-NOS, nonverbal learning disorders, social anxiety, learning disabilities and delays* [DVD]. Rockville, MD: Author.
Models social skills such as using tact, appropriate voice modulation, good hygiene, asking for help, sense of humor, and more.

Myles, B. S. (2005). *Difficult moments for children and youth with autism spectrum disorders* [DVD]. Shawnee Mission, KS: Autism Asperger Publishing.
A DVD focused on dealing with the difficult moments of a child with autism including, rumbling and rage stages, and recovery stages.

Talking Child. (2004). *Baby babble* [DVD]. Maple Grove, MN: Author.
A speech enhancing DVD specifically for babies and toddlers to begin to learn how to babble and speak.

World Class Communication Technologies (Firm), MacLean, B. N. (Executive Producer), & Luchtman, K. (Producer). (2004). *Family to family: A guide to living life when a child is diagnosed with an autism spectrum disorder* [DVD]. Higganum, CT: Starfish Specialty Press.
A family centered informational DVD that gives great insight to sharing life with a child who has autism.

American Psychiatric Association. (1994). *Diagnostic and statistical manual of mental disorders* (4th ed.). Washington, DC: Author.

Arick, J. R., Loos, L., Falco, R., & Krug, D. A. (2004). *The STAR program: Strategies for teaching based on autism research.* Austin, TX: Pro-Ed.

Arnwine, B. (2007). *Starting sensory integration therapy.* Arlington, TX: Future Horizons.

Asperger, H. (1991). "Autistic psychopathy" in early childhood. In U. Frith (Ed. & Trans.), *Autism and Asperger syndrome* (pp. 37–92). Cambridge, UK: Cambridge University Press. (Original work published 1944)

Bondy, A., & Frost, L. (2002). *A picture's worth: PECS and other visual communication strategies in autism.* Bethesda, MD: Woodbine House.

Catlett, S. M. (2007, August). *De-mystifying applied behavior analysis (ABA).* Workshop conducted for Belton ISD, Belton, TX.

Centers for Disease Control and Prevention. (2008). *Autism information center.* Retrieved January 30, 2009, from http://cdc.gov/ncbddd/autism/faq_prevalence.htm.

Coleman, M. (2005). *The neurology of autism*. New York: Oxford University Press.

Exkorn, K. S. (2005). *The autism sourcebook: Everything you need to know about diagnosis, treatment, coping and healing*. New York: Collins.

Greenspan, S. I., & Wieder, S. (2006). *Engaging autism: Using the Floortime approach to help children relate, communicate, and think*. Cambridge, MA: De Capo Press.

Ivey, J. K. (2007). Outcomes for students with autism spectrum disorders: What is important and likely according to teachers? *Education and Training in Developmental Disabilities, 42*(1), 3–13.

Kanner, L. (1943). Autistic disturbances of affective contact. *The Nervous Child, 2,* 217–250.

King, B. (2004). *Music therapy: Another path to learning and communication for children on the autism spectrum*. Arlington, TX: Future Horizons.

Koegel, R. L., & Koegel, L. K. (2006). *Pivotal response treatments for autism*. Baltimore, MD: Brookes.

Kuhlman, K., & Schweinhart, L. J. (1999). *Timing in child development*. Ypsilanti, MI: High/Scope Educational Research Foundation.

Luiselli, J. K., Russo, D. C., Christian, W. P., & Wilczynski, S. M. (2008). *Effective practices for children with autism: Educational and behavioral support interventions that work*. New York: Oxford University Press.

Mesibov, G. B., Shea, V., & Schopler, E. (2006). *The TEACCH approach to autism spectrum disorders*. New York: Springer Science+Business Media, LLC.

National Research Council. (2001). *Educating children with autism*. Washington, DC: National Academy Press.

Neisworth, J. T., & Wolfe, P. S. (2005). *The autism encyclopedia*. Baltimore: Brookes.

Shaffer, R. J., Jacokes, L. E., Cassily, J. F., Greenspan, S. I., Tuchman, R. F., & Stemmer, P. J. (2001). Effect of interactive metronome rhythmicity training on children with

ADHD. *The American Journal of Occupational Therapy, 55,* 155–162.

Taub, G. E., McGrew, K. S., Keith, T. Z. (2007). Improvements in interval time tracking and effects on reading achievement. *Psychology in the Schools, 44,* 849–863.

About the Author

Julie K. Ivey is a licensed school psychologist and an assistant professor of educational psychology at Baylor University. Her research focuses on family systems and early identification for individuals with autism spectrum disorders (ASD). She is the founder and director of the Baylor Autism Center. In addition, she trains professionals who work with individuals with ASD, specifically in the field of school psychology.

Printed in the United States
by Baker & Taylor Publisher Services